The Power of Voice in AI Writing

Practical Strategies for Business Communication

A COMPUTERS & TECHNOLOGY 2-HOUR SHORT READ

Christine Masters-Wheeler, Ph.D.

Purslane Media

ISBN 979-8-9896760-4-0

for Lukasz and Kasia

CONTENTS

What Does AI Writing Sound Like?

With recent advances in artificial intelligence, the internet is being flooded with AI-generated writing—and much of it is starting to sound the same. No matter how advanced generative AI language models get, they can't fully replicate uniquely human writing voices. Generative AI apps may provide us with writing shortcuts, but the resulting copy can come across as generic, bland, and unappealing to readers who want to engage with authentic content. If your blog posts, landing pages, emails, reports, and video scripts sound like they have been written by AI, you might lose your audience's attention.

As an English professor who specializes in writing and technology, I was excited to learn about the recent advances in generative AI. In my college classes, I have encouraged students to experiment with AI writing tools, as long as they don't rely on apps to do all the work for them. Too often, however, students try to get away with submitting AI-generated text as their own writing without applying the concepts covered in class and without doing much critical thinking. Because I am familiar with my students' writing voices, I usually can spot when they try to pass off AI-generated texts as their own. But AI-generated text lacks something that even the most imperfect student writing has: a human voice. Writing produced by AI may be technically proficient, but it lacks a sense of human presence.

If you use apps like ChatGPT frequently, you may start to notice certain canned patterns in the output. The same words show up over and over, as do common sentence and paragraph structures. These stylistic choices that generative AI models make when producing texts depend on training data from existing human writing, yet the resulting text sounds less than human. AI-generated writing lacks a sense of human presence, and this sense of presence is a key component of what we understand as "voice" in writing.

While it can be difficult to be absolutely sure if a piece of writing has been generated by AI, I have noticed some clues that have to do with word choice, marketing copywriting formulas, and excessive use of adjectives. Note that I use ChatGPT in these examples, yet I realize that other apps based on large language models (LLMs) may have their own quirks.

Clue #1: Repeated Words and Phrases

I have been keeping a list of common words and phrases that pop up often in my use of ChatGPT. Here are a few:

"delve in"
"dive in"
"leverage"
"harness"

"In a ____ world where..."

"In a ____ realm where..."

"Whether you're ____, ____, or ____, you..."

"ever-evolving"

"landscape"

"juxtaposition of ____ and ____"

In particular, ChatGPT seems to favor the words "delve," "leverage," and "harness." Before I started experimenting with ChatGPT, I never really noticed these words. If they occurred in articles, books, websites, or whatever I was reading, they didn't draw my attention. However as soon as I spent some time interacting with ChatGPT, these repeated words started to catch my eye and stand out as odd. Why is ChatGPT always telling everyone to delve, to leverage, and to harness?

You can spot websites that use generative AI by scanning for words like these. Go to a web page, use your browser's "Find" command, and scan through the page.

I have noticed that software as a service (SAAS) company landing pages and blogs especially tend to include a lot of AI-sounding copy. For example, I came across a single blog post on an SAAS company's website that includes two uses of "delve," nine uses of "leverage," and two uses of "leveraging." Granted, the post is pretty long (around 7,000 words), and so the thirteen instances of these words may not be that statistically significant. Yet, I can't help but think a human author would use these particular words less often.

Clue #2: Marketing Copywriting Formulas

Sentence patterns that resemble marketing copywriting formulas may be a tip-off that writing is AI-generated. For example, ChatGPT created the following paragraph after I asked it to write about "voice" while imitating my voice. In my prompt, I also provided a sample of my writing as a voice model. ChatGPT's output leaves much to be desired:

> In a world where AI-generated content is becoming more and more common, the importance of having a unique voice in your writing has never been clearer. Whether you're blogging, writing a novel, or just crafting an email, your voice is what sets you apart from the crowd. It's what makes your writing not just readable, but memorable.

Even though I thought my prompt was fairly well-written, this output was definitely unlike my voice sample. The blurb not only uses "ChatGPT-speak" sorts of words, but it also includes a canned pattern that is similar to many other AI outputs and resembles a marketing copywriting formula. This result is not surprising, considering that ChatGPT probably was trained on text scraped from thousands of websites that contain marketing copy.

The above output resembles two of the more well-known marketing copywriting frameworks: AIDA (attention, interest, desire, action) and PAS (problem, agitate, solution). The blurb contains an introductory sentence that poses a problem and attracts attention ("in a world...,"), a body sentence that gets the reader thinking about their interests or desires ("whether you're"), and a concluding sentence that explains an actionable solution, (the use of voice in writing).

If you are writing actual marketing copy and you don't care that it sounds like marketing copy, you could prompt for formulas like AIDA or PAS intentionally or just leave ChatGPT to do what it normally does. To avoid these constructions, you could prompt AI not to use marketing copywriting formulas.

Clue #3: Over-the-Top Adjectives

Another sign of AI-generated writing is the use of flowery or overly expressive adjectives in places that don't quite make sense. For example, consider a fitness equipment company landing page that includes a blurb about products for home gyms. To me, this text comes across as AI-generated.

In the boundless universe of personal wellness, every home gym is a sanctuary of strength and transformation. We appreciate the diverse spectrum of fitness journeys, which is why we provide a myriad of tailored equipment options. Discover countless ways to customize and elevate your workout haven according to your unique goals and aspirations.

This blurb follows a marketing copywriting framework, which in itself is not an indicator of AI use. However, the phrases "boundless universe," "diverse spectrum of fitness journeys," and "myriad of tailored equipment options" somehow have an odd, not-quite-human ring to them given the context. I could be wrong, of course—this copy could have been entirely human-written. Unfortunately, because

AI-detection apps are unreliable, there's no way to tell for sure. This blurb could have been authored by a human, an AI app, or a combination of the two.

If I were writing copy for this landing page, I would not use so many colorful adjectives. I would use more direct and relatable language. For example, "We provide a myriad of tailored options," could be written instead as, "We tailor our product options to your individual needs." This revision would make the copy come across as more authentically human, even though the more creative-sounding adjectives are missing.

How the Concept of Voice Helps

Developing a sense of human voice in writing is important even when a neutral, professional tone is desired. We have to balance AI writing shortcuts with human choices and insights. AI can be a useful writing tool, but it shouldn't be a full replacement for our own words. AI text generators can save us time when brainstorming, summarizing, drafting, and editing—but writing will always be a skill that needs to be learned and practiced. Viewing writing through the lens of voice can help everyday professionals experiment with AI while improving their writing skills.

If you take the time to develop your own writing voice, you'll better engage readers who want to feel that a real person is behind the text. Of course, there are types of writing where a strong individual presence is not desirable—for example, in a company's annual report or in a set of technical instructions. But even then, the reader should have a sense that there is a human being or a group of humans behind the words. A company's brand voice should still convey human presence.

Although voice has many possible definitions and connotations, I approach the term simply as a sense of human presence in writing or communication. Of course, sometimes this sense of human presence can be deep faked. AI-generated text, video avatars, and synthetic voices sometimes pass the Turing test. Yet, I think that more often than not, audiences still can sense when something isn't quite authentically human.

I wrote this book to help bring more humanity into AI-assisted writing. I discuss strategies for everyday professionals who want to experiment with AI without sounding like AI. Even though the topic of voice can quickly become theoretical, I hope to approach voice in an accessible and non-academic way. I aim to explain how voice comes across not only through surface-level features but also through the meanings and ideas conveyed in writing.

This book is for anyone who wants to use generative AI tools while retaining a sense of human presence in their writing. It is for entrepreneurs, sales professionals, marketing copywriters, managers, executives as well as students getting ready to enter the workforce. Really, it's for anyone who wants to use AI with integrity.

I also hope that my arguments about voice will convince decision makers that good writing matters for business. Generative AI apps are a poor substitute for human perception and judgement, especially when it comes to writing and communication. You can't just replace your writers with AI apps, but AI tools can be helpful when used well.

The following chapters explore voice as an important concept for writing, provide exercises for identifying voice, and present a framework that will help you convey an authentic human presence as you use generative AI.

Key Points

- Over-reliance on AI-generated text in professional communications can make writing sound impersonal.
- Individuals can learn to use AI while keeping a sense of human voice in their writing.
- Even though AI tools can be useful, we still need to understand writing principles and grow our writing skills.

CHAPTER ONE

Understanding Voice

Using AI to generate text can have benefits—AI can help us brainstorm, find the right words, and experiment with how to structure ideas. However, to get the most out of AI writing tools, we first need to understand some basic writing concepts, including voice. This chapter explains what the concept of voice means, discusses why it matters, and provides strategies to become more aware of our own individual writing voices as well as the ways that AI-generated writing might affect a company's brand voice.

Defining Voice

In the *Writing Commons* reference website, Joe Moxley defines voice as "a metaphorical term that refers to the unique way a writer or speaker presents their thoughts and feelings," and the "quality, style, or tone of a piece that makes a work distinct from others." There are many elements involved in voice, including the way a writer conveys tone and persona to give readers a sense of authenticity. Creative writing handbooks encourage writers to "develop their craft" and find their unique voice that sets them apart from other writers. Another sense of the term has to do with grammar, when voice is associated with active or passive types of sentence construction. Voice in writing also can simply indicate a sense of human presence. However, you don't need a distinctly creative or crafted style to convey a sense of voice in your writing.

The definition of voice as a sense of human presence is relevant especially in the age of AI. The key question these days is: Do we believe that a human is behind a piece of writing, or don't we? When voice comes through in my writing, my reader gets a sense that I am human.

> *You don't need a distinctly creative or crafted style to convey a sense of voice in your writing.*

A certain persona—a representation of who is communicating—will always come across in writing. Personas can be found in a range of genres, from emails and business reports to short stories and novels. Sometimes a writerly persona will be very specific, seeming almost like a fictional character, and sometimes the individual qualities of the persona will be generic or downplayed, like in the style of some business documents. Regardless of the context, readers get a sense of a persona's voice through its stylistic features and tone.

The concept of voice naturally resonates with most people. Even though voice can be hard to define objectively, humans have a sense for what it means. Everyone grows up surrounded by speech. The way we express ourselves becomes shaped by languages and dialects. The way I speak becomes a part of who I am—yet I can choose to speak differently depending on where I am, who I am speaking to, and what I want to achieve. Just like my handwriting has distinct curves and slants that set it apart from someone else's, my speaking voice has unique intonations to distinguish me from others. It is natural for some of our speaking voices to come through in our writing voices.

While the idea of voice may seem like common-sense, academics have critiqued the concept. Peter Elbow (2007) in "Voice in Writing Again: Embracing Contraries," points out problems that some writing scholars have had with the idea of voice.

Some academics say that voice is a confusing and misleading term. They argue that teaching the use of personal voice makes students think that good writing is just about self-expression and doesn't require critical thinking. Also, voice had been at one time associated with a way of teaching writing that encouraged students to explore their "true selves." Yet, not all writing is about self-discovery; writers express different personas depending on what they want to accomplish. Critics also argue that a strong writerly voice limits or biases how people interpret a text, which contradicts the need for neutrality and objectivity in business and scientific writing.

Countering these objections, Elbow explains that a strong voice can make a text more interesting and easier to understand. Voice can help to engage readers and make arguments more convincing. Writing in an authentic voice does not necessarily mean writing from the perspective of your so-called inner self. When we write, we can choose to reveal or not reveal information about ourselves in any number of ways while still coming across as genuine.

Elbow's (1994) introduction to *Landmark Essays on Voice and Writing* discusses five senses of voice:

1. Audible voice or intonation (the sounds of a text)
2. Dramatic voice (the character or implied author of a text)
3. Recognizable or distinctive voice
4. Voice with authority
5. Resonant voice or presence

One of the most meaningful ways to understand voice, according to Elbow, is through the concept of resonant voice or presence. It is the least objectively definable sense of voice (and because of that, he calls it "the swamp"). Resonant voice involves unconscious reactions on the part of the reader. When readers hear resonant voice or presence, they get a feel for a text's authenticity based on how it matches their ideas of the writer as a person. Resonant voice also involves the reader making judgements about the appropriateness of a piece of text for certain situations and genres. I am in the process of writing a more in-depth, academic article that addresses Elbow's other categories as they relate to AI writing. In this short guide, I focus on resonant voice because it can help us understand how we perceive voice in everyday writing with AI.

Resonant Voice

Resonant voice is an essential writing concept for the age of AI. However, I would argue that now we don't necessarily need to know anything about an author's personal identity to judge for authentic human voice. We judge authenticity based on whether the writing has what we perceive as human versus AI qualities.

Now, more than ever, people are looking for authenticity when engaging with online content. The idea of resonant voice addresses this need to perceive authenticity, or authentic human presence. Some people associate human presence with a sense of soul. It's not always possible to pinpoint exactly why we detect something as written by AI, but oftentimes we can tell because there's no resonant voice in the writing. AI writing and avatars can come across as being soulless or empty.

The perception of voice goes beyond the surface qualities of writing, including stylistic features, tone (the attitude or emotion conveyed), register (the level of formality or informality), and other similar elements. It includes the sense that the writer has unique thoughts about the topic at hand. A human voice expresses nuanced ideas, solves problems critically, and draws attention to specifics. Human writing is also more likely to include opinions and feelings on a topic. For example, I could ask an AI app to explain the qualities of a good vacation. It would describe a list of generic qualities that are transferable across many contexts. However, if I write my own explanation of the qualities of a good vacation in my original writing, it is more likely to be clear that I have certain preferences or biases, even if I don't write in the first person.

When I write, even if I take care to leave out personal opinions and preferences, I am likely to show my humanness in some way. I might make surface-level mistakes and not adhere to the paragraph formulas that AI likes to use. (For example, AI favors the "paragraph sandwich" style: topic sentence, supporting details, concluding sentence.) I am also more likely to include specific details such as place names in my writing.

There's not any one factor that distinguishes AI presence versus human presence in writing. Rather, a combination of surface-level and thinking-related qualities creates a sense of human voice.

A combination of surface-level and thinking-related qualities creates a sense of human voice in writing.

Why Voice Matters

Recently, authenticity has become a popular internet search term. When people watch YouTube or TikTok videos, they want to get a sense of a speaker's personality and authenticity. This idea of authenticity is closely related to voice. Your voice is what makes you unique. When your audience senses your authenticity through your voice, they feel that you have credibility. Audiences sense authenticity when your writing matches the way you present yourself in specific contexts. Consistency of voice shows that you are genuine and trustworthy.

Even when you are writing to represent a company and you aren't using the first person "I," readers should get the impression that a human, not an AI agent, is conveying the message. If your writing sounds generic or automated, a barrier comes between you and your readers.

Voice matters because it can powerfully represent a company or brand. For businesses, having a consistent voice across all communications creates a recognizable and reliable image. For example, a clear and consistent voice can reinforce the company's identity and values across its various content, including web copy, customer service emails, and internal memos. The concept of brand voice also can apply to individuals. You might want to convey a sense of personal brand in your writing voice that reflects your professional identity.

Voice can be adapted to suit different audiences and purposes. For example, the tone of a casual email to a colleague will differ from the tone of a formal report to a client. You can adjust the way your voice comes across depending on the circumstances.

In some cases, businesses use AI avatars or voices to deliver information. It is getting to the point where these avatars are almost indistinguishable from live recordings of humans. Does it matter whether an AI avatar or a human conveys content to audiences? After all, using AI can save money. Using text-to-video software can be cheaper than hiring actors to record marketing content. When I ask my friends and colleagues what they think, they say that it matters a lot. People can get turned off to messages that sound like they have been created by AI or seem to be delivered by AI. Companies looking to save money on content creation should get audience feedback and be strategic in determining what kinds of content are better delivered with an authentic human versus an avatar.

Voice is important in the age of AI. When you write AI prompts, having one or more samples of your voice style can help AI match how you ultimately want to come across.

What's My Authentic Voice?

This book so far has discussed voice as the feeling of human presence that gets conveyed to the reader. So, how do you know what your voice is? Can you have more than one voice? Isn't voice just for creative writing?

Voice isn't something that only fiction authors need to be successful. Everyday business professionals and anyone else who writes with AI also should consider the concept of voice. Whether you are communicating with people you know or those you don't know, they can sense when your words are not your own. When using AI tools, you should ensure that your writing sounds natural and human. Your authentic writing voice is anything you can imagine yourself writing to a specific audience that feels natural or appropriate given the context.

Still, the idea of "what feels natural" can be complicated. Many of us learn in school that the speech that actually comes naturally to us—the vernaculars that we learn to speak as a child—are not good enough for writing. In English classes, we are told that the acceptable way of writing has very strict rules. As we progress through the grades, we get the idea that our writing should be more official and proper than how we would verbally express ourselves in conversation.

But following the rules doesn't always feel natural. Rules about where to put commas or when to capitalize nouns are not very intuitive to most people. Maybe that's why AI text generators are so appealing to students who are learning academic writing. If you have been told throughout your schooling that your way of writing (and sometimes speaking) is deficient, then using AI could be a useful shortcut for conforming with the rules of Standard English. Unfortunately, even though AI text generators can produce "correct" writing on the surface-level, they also can leave out a sense of human voice.

As a writing professor, I strive to teach my students how to effectively reach their audiences. In many situations, readers will be able to better understand writing when it follows Standard English grammar and punctuation rules. Messages come across more clearly when you use active verbs and structure sentences concisely. In business settings, clear, concise communication can give your writing authority and weight. However, even as we put writing guidelines into practice, we shouldn't completely lose touch with our speaking voices.

Your speaking voice can be different from your writing voice—yet you can choose what degree your speaking voice comes across in your writing voice. In this book, for example, I've made the choice to use contractions (I'm, I've, It's) because I want to convey a sense of informality to my readers. I wouldn't use contractions if I were writing an article for a scholarly journal.

So, depending on the circumstances, it may make sense to adapt to what feels unnatural, especially when it comes to surface level features of writing. For example, the comma placement rules feel strange to a lot of people. Yet, commas help get your message across because they improve clarity. Audiences have come to expect them as a sign of polished, professional writing. The same could be said for the capitalization of proper nouns, use of topic sentences, use of transitions between ideas, and so forth. Writing conventions and style systems can help your readers better understand your message. Guidelines such as Plain Language and Simplified Technical English also can vastly improve the readability and effectivness of writing.

However, the best way to improve your writing skills is to practice expressing nuanced ideas in your own voice. While AI can edit your draft and mimic voice at the surface level, it cannot replace the sense of voice that comes from human thought.

Using AI in the wrong way will sacrifice your voice. If you start excessively copying and pasting AI-generated text into your documents, your writing will lose its sense of human presence. To avoid this problem, I offer a framework for keeping voice in AI-assisted writing in the following chapter.

References

Elbow, P. (1994). *Landmark essays on voice and writing.*

Elbow, P. (2007). Reconsiderations: Voice in writing again: Embracing contraries. *College English,* 70(2), 168-188.

Moxley, J. (2023). Voice. *Writing Commons.* https://writing-commons.org/section/rhetoric/rhetorical-stance/voice/

Key Points

- You don't need a distinctly creative or crafted style to convey a sense of voice in your writing.
- Peter Elbow's concept of *resonant voice* is the least objectively definable sense of voice, but it takes on new relevance in the age of AI.
- The idea of resonant voice speaks to the sense of authenticity that people are looking for when engaging with online content.
- Your authentic writing voice is anything you can imagine yourself writing to a specific audience that feels natural or appropriate for that context.

CHAPTER TWO

AI Writing, Human Voice

AI can help you experiment with the different ways your voice comes across to your readers in terms of style and tone. AI can show you, for example, different revisions of a writing sample that you can then "try on" to see if they fit your sense of voice. This chapter explores some of these techniques and also gives a brief overview of some key writing terms. It also covers three distinct methods that can help you keep a sense of human presence in your AI-assisted writing.

Developing a Voice Sample

This exercise uses AI to develop a sample that you can later use when you ask AI to create output using your voice.

STEP 1: RECORD YOUR VOICE

Record yourself with an app on your phone. There are a few ways to do this. You can use the microphone feature in an app that supports voice-to-text, for example Gmail. Don't write anything down. Just speak into the recording. Resist the urge to edit your transcription now. Try to speak for at least 30-60 seconds on any topic. Below are some possible questions you can record yourself answering. These prompts correspond with the three types of communication purposes from classical rhetoric: to persuade, to inform, and to entertain.

Inform

- Describe your favorite vacation spot and why you love it.
- Explain a typical day at your job or school.
- Share how you prepare your favorite meal or recipe.
- Discuss a hobby you enjoy and how you got started with it.
- Provide some tips on how to stay organized in daily life.

Persuade

- Argue why your favorite TV show or movie is worth watching.
- Convince someone to visit your hometown or a place you love.
- Explain why a certain type of music or band is the best.
- Persuade someone to try a new activity or sport that you enjoy.

Entertain

- Share a funny or memorable incident from a family gathering.
- Describe a dream you've had that was particularly interesting or weird.
- Talk about a prank you've pulled or witnessed.

- Recount an amusing or unexpected encounter you've had with a stranger.

STEP 2: TRANSCRIBE YOUR VOICE

Locate your voice recording and transcribe it to text. If you used voice-to-text, you'll have the transcript already. Otherwise, find an app that transcribes audio or do an internet search for "how to make a transcript from audio" and follow the steps provided. Check and correct any interpretative errors in the transcript—sometimes apps understand your voice as saying a different word than what you actually said.

STEP 3: GET AI FEEDBACK

Prompt AI to critique your written draft and give you three possible ways to revise it while keeping your original voice. AI will insert punctuation for you.

Prompt

I would like you to act as a writing consultant. Give me feedback on a transcript of my voice recording and offer three possible revisions. Keep the suggested revisions as close to my original voice as possible, using the same tone, style, and register. Explain your suggestions.

STEP 4: REFLECT AND REFINE

Speak aloud the AI-suggested revisions and determine which one, if any, sounds the most like something you would say. Which option sounds most natural to you? If there's one AI-generated result that is close but not quite "you," then keep revising it until it sounds like something you would say. Or, use the original transcript of your recording and only change a few words based on the ideas you get from the AI suggestions.

Once you have come up with a writing sample that you think accurately represents your voice, save it for future use. You can prompt AI to use this sample as a model when generating new texts in your voice. You might save several different snippets that serve as samples of your voice for various writing purposes. For example, you could have an informal voice sample that you use for everyday communication and a more formal voice sample that you use for writing professional documents. Or you could save different voice samples for when you want to sound entertaining, one that's more informative, and one that's more persuasive.

When you use these voice samples in your prompts, remember that AI still will not be able to replicate the thinking needed to produce a full sense of human voice. But if the prompt works well, at least the AI-generated text will sound closer to your voice.

Prompting Strategies

Here are some example prompts you can use with your own voice sample or another voice sample that you want to emulate. Change the descriptions in the brackets to suit your needs.

CLONE YOURSELF

When using this prompt, you would change the descriptions in the brackets depending on what type of document you were producing as well as your audience and purpose. You'll also specify how you want the document to sound.

Please write [a short, friendly email to customers, inviting them to our upcoming product launch event]. Use the same voice as the following paragraph:

VOICE SAMPLE: [Insert your writing sample here]

Make sure the [email] reflects the same style, voice, and register as the provided paragraph. Do not incorporate the content matter of the voice sample, just mirror the surface features. Use placeholders for any information that you don't have.

DESCRIBE A SAMPLE STYLE

Use this prompt to describe the style of any text.

Analyze the following text and then give me a set of instructions I can use to write in the same tone, style, register, reading level, and with a similar delivery. [Insert a few paragraphs of a text that you want to use as a model.]

When you have these instructions, ask AI to follow them when you are working on a new piece of writing. If you are using ChatGPT, you can create a customized GPT or use one that someone else already has saved for public use. Other AI text generation apps also may have similar settings to customize outputs.

COPY A BRAND VOICE

Another approach involves imitating a company's writing style or brand voice. AI apps that are connected to the internet can access information on brand voice and generate similar-sounding text.

> Write a [social media post] [announcing our new partnership]. Model the voice and style on [a company's] brand voice. When you write the [social media post], insert placeholders for any information you don't have. [Optional: You can also include a few paragraphs of the other company's web copy as a brand voice model as in the Clone Yourself prompt.]

Remember to edit the text to refine the sense of human voice in the final copy. I recommend reading the AI outputs aloud, sentence by sentence, and revising to match with what you think you would actually say or write. After you read a sentence aloud, pause and ask yourself whether that sounded like something you could imagine saying to someone. If not, write down alternate ways of phrasing the same idea until your writing feels more natural and suitable for your audience and purpose.

Audience, Purpose, and Genre

As with any kind of writing, it is important to be aware of a few general principles that can significantly improve the quality and effectiveness of your work when you write with AI. As you draft your message, be clear about who you are writing to, why you are writing, and what the expectations are for the genre or type of writing you are doing. If you have ever taken a writing class, you are likely to recognize audience, genre, and purpose as *rhetorical* terms.

Understanding your audience is crucial because it influences the tone, language, and content of your message. If you are writing to a colleague, a casual tone may be appropriate. However, if your audience is a client or a senior executive, a more formal tone would likely be better received. Consider the audience's level of knowledge about the topic. Are they experts who need detailed technical information, or are they laypeople who would benefit from simpler explanations?

To understand purpose, be clear about what you are trying to achieve with your writing. Are you trying to inform, persuade, request, educate, or provide instructions? Defining your goal helps to shape your writing and ensures that your message is focused and effective. For example, if you want your audience to take some specific action after reading your email, you should make sure your request is clear and provide all relevant information. If you are writing a report to convey information, check that your data is presented clearly and logically, with a well-supported conclusion.

Also consider the type of document you are composing. Every genre has its own conventions and expectations. For example, an email typically has a specific format: a greeting, a concise body, and a closing. It's meant to be direct and to the point, often used for quick communication. On the other hand, a letter, though similar, often carries a more formal tone and may include more detailed explanations and specific page layouts. Reports are even more structured—they often include sections such as an introduction, methodology, findings, and conclusion. You'll make choices about whether you are writing in the first person or third person, the kinds of language you use, and so on, depending on the genre or type of document you are producing.

You can analyze any piece of writing for audience, genre, and purpose. Take this book, for example. In the introduction, I define my audience and purpose. My audience is business professionals, and my purpose is to help them improve their AI writing strategies by understanding voice. The genre of this book is a business writing handbook geared towards popular rather than academic markets.

Understanding these three elements—genre, audience, and purpose—can help you approach any type of writing with more confidence and clarity. When you keep these aspects of writing in mind, you will produce writing that is not only more effective but also more engaging and tailored to your specific context. This will ultimately help you communicate more effectively and achieve your goals, whether in emails, reports, or in any other form of writing.

Three Methods for Writing with AI

To keep a sense of human presence in your writing, use one of these three AI-assisted writing methods. Each has strengths and weaknesses, and each involves work on the part of the writer.

1. Human-First Draft
2. AI-Outlined Draft
3. AI-First Draft

The sections below give a general overview and introduction to each method. Detailed scenarios and prompts for the three methods follow in later chapters.

METHOD 1: HUMAN-FIRST DRAFT

With this method, you simply write a draft and then use AI as a writing coach. However, it is important to be specific in the ways you ask AI for feedback. You should tell the AI tool about your genre, audience, and purpose, thus taking a rhetorical approach to the revisions. This process can involve going through several iterations where you will consider different ways to organize your ideas. When you are working with longer passages, AI can make summary outlines of your paragraphs and suggest how to better organize the flow of ideas. As you rewrite your original draft, you'll make all the revisions in your own words. Once you are satisfied with the revisions, you can ask AI to proofread for spelling and grammatical errors.

METHOD 2: AI-OUTLINED DRAFT

In this approach, you write a prompt that provides AI with your genre, audience, and purpose as well as a request to create an outline of your draft. You also can ask AI to suggest a first sentence (topic sentence) for each paragraph. Then, copy and paste these suggested outlines or topic sentences into a new document and fill in content for the paragraphs. After expanding the outline with your own writing, you can use AI to offer revision suggestions (see Method 1). Once you are happy with your draft, you can ask AI to proofread for spelling and grammatical errors.

METHOD 3: AI-FIRST DRAFT

Here, you ask AI to write something for you, but then rewrite the output as needed to align with your desired voice. You'll first write a prompt asking AI to write in a specific genre for a defined audience and purpose. Next, you'll make substantial revisions to make the output sound like something you would say or write.

This method involves analyzing the AI-generated output sentence by sentence and experimenting with variations. If you use this method, you'll also want to notice places where AI has made vague generalizations and rewrite the text to include relevant examples and deeper thinking. If AI has provided specific examples or has cited other works, be aware that these references could be fake or inaccurate. You must fact-check everything that AI generates.

At first glance, this AI-drafted approach may seem like

the least amount of work, but done well, it can end up taking a lot of time.

If you are using Method 3, there are a few different approaches to prompting that specifically address the concept of voice. You can make the AI output sound closer to your voice or a specific brand voice that you want to use as a model. However, keep in mind, that regardless of how well you craft a prompt for a desired voice, AI-generated outputs need to be reviewed and revised to come across as human.

Key Points

- Carefully edit and revise all AI-generated texts to make sure AI outputs sound human and match the intended style.
- Before you write anything, you should be able to answer these questions to streamline your writing processes:

  Who is my audience? What is their frame of mind?

  What sort of tone will my audience best respond to?

  What is the genre?

  What do people expect from this kind of document?

  What is the purpose? Why am I writing?

- This book presents three methods for AI-assisted writing: Human-First Draft, AI-Outlined Draft, and AI-First Draft.
- When using Method 3, you can use voice samples for personalization.

CHAPTER THREE

Content Writing with AI

Across many industries, businesses have been using AI tools to produce online content. Conveying a consistent brand voice is important for content. AI can help with this, but we still need to ensure that brand voice reflects human presence so that "AI-speak" doesn't take over.

While there are many facets to content writing, I cover only a few in this chapter. In the first sections, I focus on how AI can assist in creating brand voice, identifying keywords, and brainstorming ideas for testing content. The last section demonstrates how to use the *Three Methods for Writing with AI* when creating a blog post.

Developing a Brand Voice

Whether you are writing content for an organization or to represent you personally, your voice should be consistent throughout all platforms. While you shouldn't rely on AI alone to determine the voice of your content, AI tools can analyze previous content samples and identify the voice that characterizes your brand. When you have a content sample that you think does a good job of reflecting your brand voice, save it as a model and ask AI to mimic this voice when generating future content. That output can be a starting point for you to further revise and make sure that the content doesn't sound like AI but instead conveys a sense of human presence.

Keep in mind that the style and tone of your content also should be adapted to the conventions of specific platforms. For example, the copy you write for a landing page will be different from that of a social media post and again be different from content in a help topic.

This section uses *Method 1: Human-First Draft* to analyze existing human-authored copy for brand voice. You can try this process with your own content or pick another company that you want to analyze for brand voice.

Most large companies, such as Starbucks or Walmart, already have sophisticated marketing strategies and they explain their brand voice on their websites, often along with their style guide. These explanations can be useful if you want to copy a brand voice as you experiment with your own content. Smaller companies and nonprofit organizations often lack a consistent a strong brand voice because they are short on resources for marketing and information design.

For this demonstration, I'm using a local county park site that advertises cabins for rent. I will prompt ChatGPT to identify the brand voice characteristics of this site and make recommendations on how to improve it.

Prompt

Imagine that you are a content design consultant. I'm interested in improving the brand voice of a website. I will provide the link to the site. I would like you to analyze the current language on the site and 1) report back a description of it, and 2) provide a list of suggestions for how to improve the brand voice. Include an example.

ChatGPT

Current Language Analysis

Tone: Informative and straightforward.

Style: Utilitarian, focused on providing clear and essential details about cabin amenities, rules, and booking procedures.

Voice: Formal, slightly impersonal, with an emphasis on practical information.

Strengths:

- Clear and concise.

- Provides all necessary information in an organized manner.

- Direct and to the point.

Weaknesses:

- Lacks personality and warmth.

- Could be more engaging and inviting.

- Minimal use of persuasive or descriptive language.

Suggestions for Improvement

1. Add Personality: Incorporate a warm, welcoming tone to make the content feel more personable and inviting.

2. *Use Descriptive Language: Enhance descriptions with sensory details to help readers visualize the experience.*

3. *Engage the Reader: Ask questions or use exclamations to draw readers in and create a sense of excitement.*

4. *Highlight Unique Features: Emphasize what makes the cabins and the park special to create a memorable impression.*

5. *Create a Consistent Brand Voice: Ensure all content aligns with the desired brand personality, whether it's adventurous, family-friendly, or serene.*

Example of Improved Content

Before: "Located near the river, each cabin can accommodate up to 6 people. Cabin 2 is handicap-accessible. Amenities include: central air/heat, refrigerator, toaster, microwave, stove, 12-cup coffee pot (filters not provided), silverware, basic pots and pans, wifi, outdoor grill, fire pit, towels, bed linens."

After: "Nestled by the serene river, our cozy cabins are the perfect getaway for up to six guests. Whether you're here to relax or explore, you'll love the comfort and convenience of our well-equipped accommodations. Each cabin features modern amenities like central air and heat, a fully stocked kitchen, and even a toasty fire pit for those cool evenings. Plus, Cabin 2 is thoughtfully designed for accessibility. Imagine sipping your morning coffee on the porch, surrounded by nature's beauty – it's the perfect start to your day at [name of park]!"

By making these adjustments, the content becomes more engaging and inviting, encouraging potential visitors to imagine themselves enjoying the experience.

The "after" web copy here could be a good starting point for developing a new brand voice for the site. To further work with this copy, I would ask ChatGPT to rewrite the blurb in various brand voices of well-known companies. I would consider the strengths and weaknesses of all the versions before revising the one I liked best. Once I arrived at an example voice blurb that I think represents the organization well, I would ask ChatGPT to write a description of its stylistic qualities. That description and the sample blurb could be used as a new brand voice description and go in the organization's style guide. To finish creating this piece of content, I would further rework the sentences, speaking aloud as I go, to make sure they sound genuine, human, and appropriate for the context.

Remember that voice is about more than stylistic features—to communicate authentic human presence, make sure the copy has depth and discusses specific details.

Researching Topics and Keywords

With content genres such as social media posts, web copy, and blog posts, keywords play a bigger role than in other types of business-related writing. Keywords are the phrases or questions that you type into a search box when looking for information online. Keywords help with search engine optimization (SEO), a process that helps search engines find the information that users are looking for. To rank and display the most relevant results for queries, search engines collect and index keywords from web pages. If you want your content to be found, it is important to identify the right keywords and integrate them naturally into your content.

While there are many companies that offer SEO services for hire, free or low-cost generative AI tools can help identify the keywords that resonate with specific audiences. For example, if you're writing for a tech-savvy audience, ChatGPT can analyze trending topics within tech forums, social media, and industry publications, uncovering the specific questions your audience is asking.

Once you identify keywords, you can ask AI to help integrate them in your existing content or create new content that includes them.

In this demonstration, I imagine that I'm writing content for a blog about podcasting. I will ask ChatGPT to search a Reddit forum on the subject, summarize the most popular subject areas, and provide some specific questions related to podcasting.

AI CHAT LOG

Prompt

I would like you to be my content writing consultant. I will give you the link to a discussion forum on a specific subject. I would like you to list the most popular topics within that subject. Then, summarize the questions that users most ask about the top two topics.

[After ChatGPT's responds that it is ready, I type in the link for the Reddit forum on podcasting (www.reddit.com/r/podcasting).]

ChatGPT

Based on my exploration of the r/podcasting subreddit, here are the most popular topics:

1. Starting a Podcast: Equipment recommendations, setup guides, and initial steps.

2. Technical Issues: Troubleshooting recording, editing, and sound quality problems.

3. Marketing and Promotion: Strategies for growing an audience and social media marketing.

4. Content Creation: Tips for engaging content, episode ideas, and guest interviews.

5. Monetization: Methods for generating revenue through sponsorships and ads.

Summary of Questions for Top Two Topics:

Starting a Podcast:

- What basic equipment do I need to start a podcast?

- How do I set up my recording space for the best sound quality?

- What are the first steps to launching my podcast on various platforms?

Technical Issues:

- How can I fix poor audio quality in my recordings?

- What software should I use for editing my podcast?

- Why is there a delay or echo in my audio, and how can I resolve it?

Feel free to ask if you need detailed information on any of these topics!

These results tell me that many forum users ask specific questions about podcasting. To drive traffic to my podcasting blog, I should create articles that answer these specific questions. ASQ Content, or content that "answers specific questions" tends to get the most traffic.

To come up with more ideas, I could ask ChatGPT to expand the search to other forums or websites. I also could ask ChatGPT to identify a list of keywords that I should incorporate into my content as I use one of the Three Methods for Writing with AI.

Blog Post with Method 1: Human-First Draft

To use this method, I would draft a blog post that answers one of the specific questions that ChatGPT uncovered in the podcasting subreddit. For example, the title of my post might be "Which equipment do I need to start a podcast?" I would write from a beginner's point of view, as if I also had just gotten started, and explain my process of researching what equipment to purchase. Before writing, I would use a site such as *Answer the Public* to research keywords that would be likely to attract traffic to my post. After writing a draft that takes reader through my decision process for what equipment to buy, I would ask ChatGPT for recommendations on how to improve my draft. I demonstrate this process below. While a full blog post would likely be at least 2,000 words, for this example, I'm only including my introduction paragraph.

AI CHAT LOG

Prompt

I would like you to act as a tutor for blog writing. I have written a blog introduction draft. I will upload the draft as well as the keywords that I wanted to incorporate in it. I would like you to give me feedback on how to improve the blog post for better audience engagement. Give me a short explanation of your rationale.

ChatGPT

Sounds great! Please go ahead and upload your blog introduction draft along with the keywords. Once I review it, I'll provide feedback on how to enhance audience engagement and explain why certain changes could improve the post.

Prompt

Post draft: I have been wanting to start a podcast about knitting, but I was clueless on how to get started. I wanted to figure out the best podcasting equipment for beginners. And as someone new to all this, I also needed to know the ins and outs of setting up podcasting equipment. I wondered if I should buy a bundle or a kit, what I should get if I wanted to do video podcasting, and what I could afford on my budget. So, I did some research. I watched a bunch of how-to guides on YouTube, asked around a podcasting subreddit, and looked up review articles and Amazon reviews for audio and video equipment. After taking all of this information in, I came up with a podcasting equipment list. I am sharing it with you, along with my reasoning for the must-have podcasting equipment needed versus what you can probably do without. I also explain the easiest way to set it all up.

Keywords used:

how to set up podcasting equipment, best podcasting equipment for beginners, podcasting equipment list, podcasting equipment needed, video podcasting bundle, budget, kit

ChatGPT

Suggested Revisions:

1. Stronger Hook: Grab attention with a benefit-focused opener. If you're like me and ready to dive into podcasting but clueless about equipment, you're in the right place.

2. Clarify the Problem/Solution: Highlight the value of your research early on. I spent hours researching the best podcasting equipment for beginners, so you don't have to. Whether it's video or audio, I've got you covered.

3. Add Structure: Break up info for readability. Should you buy a bundle? What's needed for video? How to stick to your budget?

4. Natural Keyword Integration: Weave keywords smoothly. In this post, I'll show you how to set up podcasting equipment easily.

5. Call to Action: Encourage the reader to continue. Let's dive in and get your podcast off the ground with the right gear!

Final Version:

If you're like me and ready to dive into podcasting but clueless about equipment, you're in the right place. I spent hours researching the best podcasting equipment for beginners, so you don't have to. Whether it's video or audio, I've got you covered.

Should you buy a bundle? What's needed for video? How to stick to your budget? In this post, I'll show you how to set up podcasting equipment easily.

Let's dive in and get your podcast off the ground with the right gear!

Why These Changes Help:

> *Hook: More engaging start.*
>
> *Clear Solution: Shows value early.*
>
> *Structure: Improves readability.*
>
> *Keywords: Better SEO integration.*
>
> *Call to Action: Keeps readers engaged.*

These updates will boost readability and audience engagement.

I appreciated ChatGPT's suggestions regarding audience attention, but I think that the suggested revision would take away my original sense of voice. I made some changes in a new draft that retained a lot of the original wording. I didn't want the post to lose a sense of my personality and leave out how I approached my research. Also, I decided not to include a call to action (CTA), since readers would naturally be moving their attention to the list that comes next.

I uploaded my revision to ChatGPT and it refined it for me again.

AI CHAT LOG

Prompt

I made some additional changes. Please give me feedback on them. Here's the new draft:

If you're like me, you have been wanting to start a podcast, but you're clueless about equipment. My expertise is in knitting (my podcast topic), not technology. You might be in the same boat. To educate myself on what I might need, I spent hours researching the best podcasting equipment for beginners. I'll share with you what I've found.

Some of my questions were: Should buy a bundle or a kit? What can I afford on my budget? How do make the audio and video work together? To answer these questions, I watched a bunch of how-to guides on YouTube, asked around a podcasting subreddit, and looked up Amazon reviews for audio and video equipment. After taking all of this information in, I came up with the best podcasting equipment list for beginners.

ChatGPT

Your revised draft has improved clarity and a more personal tone, which is great for engaging your audience. Here's some feedback on how to refine it even further:

Feedback:

Personalize the hook more: You already have a great, relatable start. Adding a bit more connection to your readers' struggles could make it stronger.

Smooth transitions: Some sentences feel abrupt, like the shift from your expertise to your research process. Adding a bridge can make the flow smoother.

Clarify your questions: The section with questions could use cleaner phrasing for readability.

Tighten the conclusion: The last sentence is clear, but simplifying it can make it punchier.

Revised Version:

If you're like me, you've been eager to start a podcast but clueless about equipment. While I'm an expert in knitting (the focus of my podcast), figuring out the tech side was a challenge. Since I'm not a tech expert, I knew I needed to do my homework. I spent hours researching the best podcasting equipment for beginners and now, I'm sharing everything I've learned.

I had questions like: Should I buy a bundle or kit? How can I stay within my budget? And how do I make sure my audio and video work together seamlessly? To get answers, I watched countless how-to guides, asked around on a podcasting subreddit, and scoured Amazon reviews for audio and video gear. After all that research, I've compiled the ultimate beginner's podcasting equipment list.

Why These Changes Help:

Hook: More personal and engaging right from the start.

Flow: Smoother transitions between ideas make it easier to read.

Clarity: Cleaning up the questions makes the post feel more polished.

Conclusion: A punchier ending leaves a stronger impact.

Your changes are heading in a great direction!

ChatGPT's feedback makes sense, but I still think that my last revision feels more like "me" even if it's true that certain aspects of the copy, like the transitions, could be improved. Some of ChatGPT's word choices, like "scoured," are not words that seem like something I would say. Still, this final version is not too far from my voice, and I would feel comfortable using it with just a few changes.

Blog Post with Method 2: AI-Outlined Draft

To write a blog post with this method, ask AI to be your writing assistant. Tell it you are writing a blog post and describe your audience and purpose. Let it know how long you want the post to be. Then, ask AI to create an outline for your blog post with a suggested topic sentence for each paragraph. If you agree with the suggestions in the output, then elaborate on the AI-generated ideas while incorporating the keywords into the draft.

AI CHAT LOG

Prompt

I would like you to be my writing assistant. I am writing a blog post to inform other beginners about what equipment to buy when starting a podcast. My blog post will be in listicle format. I would like you to write an outline for the post and suggest topic sentences for each paragraph or section before the listicle.

ChatGPT

Introduction:

  • *Introduce the importance of starting with the right podcast equipment.*

45

- *Highlight how overwhelming it can be for beginners to decide what gear to buy.*

Suggested Topic Sentence:

"Starting a podcast can feel overwhelming, especially when it comes to choosing the right equipment, but with a few basics, you'll be ready to record like a pro."

Section 1: Determining Your Podcasting Needs

- *Assess your recording space, budget, and style (solo or with guests).*
- *Set realistic expectations for gear based on your podcast's goals.*

Suggested Topic Sentence:

"Before you start shopping for equipment, it's important to consider your podcasting setup—whether you're recording solo, with guests, or on the go."

Section 2: Essential Podcasting Equipment Checklist

- *Introduce the listicle format.*
- *Explain that you'll be covering essential items that beginners should prioritize.*

Suggested Topic Sentence:

"Here's a simple checklist of essential podcasting equipment that every beginner should consider."

This outline could be useful to remind me of what to include in my blog post. However, the tone is not quite my style. I can't imagine saying the phrases "record like a pro" or "whether you're recording solo, with guests, or on the go." To keep my sense of voice intact, I would rewrite the topic sentences in my own words.

Blog Post with Method 3: AI-First Draft

If I were using Method 3, I would give ChatGPT the genre, audience, and purpose along with a list of keywords to incorporate in an AI-generated draft. I also would tell it to use my voice sample as a model for the output's tone, style, and register.

AI CHAT LOG

Prompt

Please write a blog post introduction. The blog will be in listicle format. The audience is people just starting out with podcasting. The purpose is to help these beginners figure out which equipment to buy.

Use these keywords in the paragraph: how to set up podcasting equipment, best podcasting equipment for beginners, podcasting equipment list, podcasting equipment needed, video podcasting, bundle, budget, kit

Use the same voice as the following paragraph:

VOICE SAMPLE: [I inserted my voice sample paragraph.]

Make sure the blog post reflects the same style, voice, and register as the provided paragraph. Do not incorporate the content matter of the voice sample, just mirror the surface features. Use placeholders for any information that you don't have.

ChatGPT

Starting a podcast can feel a little overwhelming, especially when you're staring at a long list of gear wondering, What do I actually need? Trust me, I've been there. Whether you're thinking about launching a simple audio podcast or diving into video podcasting, it's easy to feel like you're drowning in options. But here's the good news: you don't need to break the bank to get started.

In this post, we'll walk through how to set up podcasting equipment without blowing your budget, covering everything from the best podcasting equipment for beginners to what kind of podcasting kit or bundle might work for you. If you're curious about what podcasting equipment is needed, whether you're going solo or collaborating with guests, this podcasting equipment list has got you covered. Let's get into it!

The tone and style of ChatGPT's output is somewhat close to the conversational voice sample I provided. Yet, the output feels generic to me. To use this AI-first draft, I will need to make some changes. For example, the "Whether you're..." sentences definitely sound canned because this construction is one that ChatGPT's repeats quite often. If I were to use this output, I would change that sentence and add in more details to give readers a sense of me as a person. Like I did in my Method 1 section draft, I would talk about what kind of podcast I am starting and where I researched the equipment options.

I could keep asking ChatGPT to refine this output—for example by instructing it not to use the "Whether you're" sentence structure. I could also experiment with feeding instructions to ChatGPT in a more segmented fashion to see if that improves the output. For example, I could ask for a draft without including the voice instructions and then ask for another revision that conforms to my voice sample. In any case, I ultimately would want to revise the output sentence by sentence to make the voice more personalized.

Beyond writing blog posts, you can use these AI writing methods for any kind of content—for example, for landing page copy, video descriptions, product descriptions, or social media posts. Remember that AI also can help you brainstorm article titles and headings, give feedback on SEO keywords, and show alternative ways to integrate keywords naturally into sentences.

Regardless of what kind of content you write and the method you use, be sure to revise for voice. Voice goes beyond phrasing; it's also about depth of discussion. Developing voice in writing means bringing in nuances and perspectives that AI is likely to miss.

Testing Content

Testing content will help ensure that it attracts, engages, and informs users. AI tools designed for marketers can assist in gathering and analyzing feedback from your audience, thereby helping you understand what works and what doesn't. Some platforms, such as Meta and YouTube, conduct A/B testing to let you know which versions of your content will be most successful.

In addition to the tests that are available within content platforms and marketing apps, you can use AI tools like ChatGPT to design user testing plans and advise you on User Experience (UX) strategies. Before you use anything that AI suggests, however, you should educate yourself on best practices by consulting reputable sources. For more about UX and ideas for integrating AI into UX processes, see the Nielsen Norman Group website (www.nngroup.com).

When prompted, ChatGPT can provide a comprehensive user testing plan to evaluate the effectiveness of new website copy. Without much prompting of what the plan should include, ChatGPT creates objectives, such steps for assessing clarity, engagement, and overall user experience. ChatGPT's proposed methodology involves a combination of usability testing, surveys, and A/B testing. The plan also outlines a timeline, from participant recruitment to final reporting, and suggests tools and resources for each testing method

This framework could be a good starting point that you would adapt to suit your available resources. For example, you could do user observations and A/B testing but skip the survey, or vice versa. You also could ask ChatGPT to help brainstorm more specifically how to carry out the individual methods. Your research questions could focus on particular aspects of the user experience—for example, finding out how users perceive voice in your content.

Key Points

- AI can help you analyze existing brand voice in in your content.
- Voice is about more than stylistic features—to communicate authentic human presence, make sure your content has depth and discusses specific details.
- AI tools can assist in identifying the keywords that resonate with particular audiences.

CHAPTER FOUR

Email Writing with AI

When you start a new job, you may notice that people in your organization follow different email conventions than what you were used to before. For example, your coworkers may have specific trends in starting an email (the salutation) and ending an email (the complimentary close). These typical patterns or trends are called genre conventions, and they can vary among companies, industries, and global regions.

In my business and technical writing classes, I teach general principles and conventions for writing different genres, such as emails and reports. However, in practice, these conventions vary depending on where you work, and genre expectations also can change over time. In any case, it's a good idea to keep the following general guidelines in mind as you write emails.

- Be specific in the subject line.
- Address the recipient by name in your salutation.
- Get to the point in the first sentence or paragraph.
- Organize paragraphs with topic sentences.
- Be brief and to-the-point.

- Include a call to action or define expectations for the recipient's next steps at the end of the email.
- Use an appropriate close.
- Customize your signature block.

Most AI apps will be able to tell you what these email conventions are and then write emails that follow them. However, it's important for you to be familiar with them as well, so you can double-check AI outputs and fill in any missing parts. You should also know how to use proper formatting and line spacing in your emails. Examples of email formats may be found in business writing reference websites or through an internet search.

Remember that when writing prompts, you should state your genre, audience, and purpose unless it is already implied. That way, AI understands the writing situation. You should also give AI a role that you want it to play.

The following example scenario is for a workplace situation where I ask a colleague to collaborate with me on a writing project.

Email with Method 1: Human-First Draft

For this email draft, I used ChatGPT 4o. The prompts and responses are below. Note that my prompts give ChatGPT the details about my genre, audience, and purpose. I ask it to play the role of a business writing tutor. I also set up the task and then tell ChatGPT to let me know when it is ready. Prompting instructions in stages can help ChatGPT output better results.

Prompt

I would like you to act as a business writing tutor. I will give you a draft of an email that I wrote. Please give me suggestions, keeping my original voice and considering the context, audience, and purpose of my email.

Context: I am working on a large report that has many sections.

Audience: I am writing to a colleague who has higher status than me but is not my boss. I have worked with this person for many years, and we have a good rapport.

Purpose: I would like the colleague to help me write a section of the report.

When you are ready, please ask me for my draft text.

ChatGPT

I'm ready to help you with your email draft. Please go ahead and share the text you have written so far.

Prompt

Here is my original email that I would like you to help with.

Subject: Student Services Report Section

Hi John,

I just left you a voicemail about this—I am wondering if you could help me fill in this part of the narrative for student services. I'm having a hard time coming up with language to describe the differences in health services locations and what they each offer to students. Would you please offer suggestions to improve this section?

Thank you in advance for your help.

Christine

ChatGPT

Your email is clear and concise, but I have a few suggestions to make it more polished and respectful, considering John's higher status:

Subject: Assistance Needed for Student Services Report Section

Hi John,

I hope this message finds you well. I left you a voicemail earlier, but I wanted to follow up with an email regarding the report we are working on. I'm currently drafting the narrative for the student services section and could use your expertise.

I'm struggling to articulate the differences between the various health services locations and what each one offers to students. Would you be able to review this section and offer any suggestions for improvement?

Your input would be invaluable, and I appreciate your assistance in advance.

Best regards,

Christine

While I liked that ChatGPT provided a bit more structure to the email, I feel like the voice is still too formal for the relationship that I have with my colleague. Rather than ask ChatGPT to revise the text again, I used ChatGPT's last output and rewrote some of the more formal parts in a more conversational tone that sounds more like me. The changes are emphasized in bold text. I made the subject and first sentence sound a bit less stuffy. I also changed some of the words to be more conversational. For example, I feel that I would be more likely to say "describe" rather than "articulate" in the first sentence of the second paragraph. Finally, I simply closed with my name instead of the more formal "Best regards" closing. Making these changes helps me keep a sense of authentic voice in the email while providing better structure and readability. The revised parts are in bold type below.

Final Edited Version

Subject: **Help with the** Student Services Report Section

Hi John,

I hope you are having a good week. I left you a voicemail earlier, but I wanted to follow up **about the report.** I'm currently drafting the narrative for the student services section and could use your expertise.

I'm struggling to **describe** the differences between the various health services locations and what each one offers to students. Would you be able to review this section and offer **your suggestions?**

Your input would **help me out a lot—thank you in advance.**

Christine

This version was not too much different from the original, but I do think that AI helped me to organize the email a bit better so that my problem (what I needed help with) stands out more. It is now the first sentence in the second paragraph. First sentences of paragraphs (topic sentences) usually draw more attention from readers than sentences that come later in a paragraph.

Email with Method 2: AI-Outlined Draft

For this draft, I also used ChatGPT 4o. Note that I still give ChatGPT the details about my context, audience, and purpose. The following chat log demonstrates how to use

ChatGPT or a similar app to help you outline an email that you will then complete in your own words.

Prompt

I would like you to act as a business writing tutor. Give me an outline for an email that I want to write. Use brackets as placeholders where I should insert relevant information. Do not write the email for me—just give me instructions and an outline for how to structure the email. Also provide topic sentences for each paragraph. Below is my context, audience, and purpose.

Context: I am working on a large report that has many sections.

Audience: I am writing to a colleague who has higher status than me but is not my boss. I have worked with this person for many years, and we have a good rapport.

Purpose: I would like the colleague to help me write a section of the report.

ChatGPT

Subject: Request for Assistance with [Specific Section] of [Report Name]

Greeting: Hi [Colleague's Name],

Paragraph 1: Introduction and Context

    Topic Sentence: I hope this email finds you well.

    [Brief pleasantries or small talk, if appropriate]

    [Mention the ongoing report and its significance]

    [Briefly state your current involvement and progress in the report]

Paragraph 2: Explanation of the Request

    Topic Sentence: I am reaching out to request your assistance with a specific section of the report.

[Specify the section of the report you need help with]

[Explain why you believe your colleague's expertise or input would be valuable]

[Mention any preliminary work or outline you have already completed for this section]

Paragraph 3: Details of the Assistance Needed

Topic Sentence: Here are the details of what I am hoping you can help with.

[Detail the specific tasks or aspects of the section you need help with]

[Provide any relevant deadlines or timelines]

[Mention if there are any resources or materials you can provide to assist them]

Paragraph 4: Offer of Support and Gratitude

Topic Sentence: Your assistance would be greatly appreciated, and I am happy to support you in return.

[Express gratitude for considering the request]

[Offer to reciprocate the help in any way you can]

[Mention your availability for further discussion or collaboration]

Closing:

Closing: Thank you in advance for your time and consideration.

[Closing remarks]

Best regards,

[Your Name]

I think that ChatGPT was overly thorough in this suggested outline. It's not necessary to have this many paragraphs in such a simple email. I would modify this outline to two paragraphs total before a closing line. I would also modify the tone to sound less formal. If I were to continue with this method, I would end up writing something close to what I had written using Method 1. Still, this method could be useful in certain situations. For example, if I were really at a loss for what to say, this method would help me to get started with writing. An outline could also remind me of what to include, so I don't forget anything and end up causing an unnecessary chain of emails back and forth to answer my recipient's questions.

Email with Method 3: AI-First Draft

This prompt contains the core instructions from Methods 1 and 2. I give ChatGPT the details about my context, audience, and purpose, but I ask it to draft the email for me.

AI CHAT LOG

Prompt

I would like you to act as a business writing tutor. Give me a draft of an email that has the following context, audience, and purpose.

Context: I am working on a large report that has many sections.

Audience: I am writing to a colleague who has higher status than me but is not my boss. I have worked with this person for many years, and we have a good rapport.

Purpose: I would like the colleague to help me write a section of the report.

ChatGPT

Subject: Assistance Needed for Upcoming Report

Hi [Colleague's Name],

I hope this email finds you well. I'm reaching out because I am currently working on a comprehensive report that encompasses multiple sections, and I could use your expertise on a particular part.

Given your extensive experience and our history of collaboration, I believe your insights would be invaluable for the [specific section or topic]. Your input would not only enhance the quality of the report but also ensure we cover all critical aspects thoroughly.

Would you be available to assist me with this? I would greatly appreciate your help and any suggestions you might have. If you have time this week, perhaps we could schedule a brief meeting to discuss it further.

Looking forward to your positive response.

Best regards,

[Your Name]

[Your Position]

[Your Contact Information]

ChatGPT's output makes all the right moves for an email, but it just doesn't feel or sound like my voice. If I were writing to someone who I needed to be very formal with, I might use this tone. To proceed with this method, I could ask ChatGPT to rewrite the output more informally, or I could recognize the purpose of each paragraph and rewrite it in my own words. Below are the results from asking ChatGPT to rewrite the draft.

Prompt

Thank you for that draft. Would you please rewrite it with a more informal voice? Here's an example of text from an original email that I wrote. Use it as a model for the kind of tone and style that I want to use.

[insert voice sample]

ChatGPT

Subject: Quick Favor for the Report?

Hi [Colleague's Name],

Hope you're doing well! I'm knee-deep in this big report, and there's a section where I could really use your magic touch.

We've worked together long enough for me to know how valuable your input is, especially for the [specific section or topic]. Think you could help me out with it? It would mean a lot, and I know it'll make the report that much better.

If you have some time this week, maybe we could chat about it and get things rolling. Let me know what works for you!

Thanks a ton,

[Your Name]

[Your Position]

[Your Contact Information]

This voice is closer to my own in terms of informality, but it still sounds "off" to me. To revise, I will go through each sentence and read it out loud, thinking of how I would actually speak this message to another person. For example, I would never say the phrase "knee-deep in this report" or the phrase "could use your magic touch." I would just say "working on this report" and "could use your help" instead. The tone of the second paragraph sounds cheesy to me and overly-flattering, so I would change that too. I might leave the closing paragraph as is, since the voice sounds somewhat like my own. However, I would take out "a ton" after "Thanks" because that seems a little over the top to me.

Ultimately, my final revision using this method would come close to the final revision that I landed on with Method 1, where I wrote the first draft of the email myself. When I reflect on what Method 3 offers, I conclude that it's good for helping me produce a quick draft. Since this particular email is not long, it won't take me much time to change the AI voice of the draft into my own voice. Then again, it didn't take me long to write the draft using Method 1 in the first place.

When compared against each other, the three methods had a similar level of effectiveness for helping me write this particular email. If I were starting from scratch and had to pick just one method, I would go with Method 2, the AI-outlined method. The outline helps me remember everything that I may want to include in the email, and I'm free to delete the parts I don't need. Working from the outline, I can personalize the message in my own voice without having to do a lot of text revisions.

If you experiment with all three methods yourself, you will find the one that works best for you.

Key Points

- Make sure that you know genre expectations when composing emails.
- Remember to tell AI its expected role, as well as the context, audience, and purpose when writing prompts.
- Each method can be effective for writing emails, but experimenting with all of them can help you figure out which method works best for you.

CHAPTER FIVE

Report Writing with AI

AI can be useful as a writing assistant for business reports or other similar documents. There are many different kinds of reports such as project reports, recommendation reports, lab reports, informational reports, white papers... and the list goes on. If you are unfamiliar with genre conventions of a certain type of report, AI apps can help. When prompted, they probably will give you a fairly accurate list of sections that should be included in a certain type of report or any other kind of business document. I have found that AI gives advice that matches the guidelines in business writing textbooks. To double-check for accuracy, you can find open-source business writing textbooks online that describe the conventions for various types of business documents.

Make sure you aren't violating any company policies that prohibit employees from sharing proprietary information with AI apps.

While AI can give you a good summary of what kinds of information should be in each report section, it is not good at writing entire reports by itself. If you ask AI to write an entire report for you from start to finish, the end product likely will be surface-level and sound inauthentic. This chapter offers strategies for keeping your voice in reports. Reports should convey a sense of human presence and also provide readers with nuanced and in-depth information.

Report Genre Conventions

When prompted to list the parts of a report, ChatGPT provides an accurate list of typical report sections and describes what goes in each section.

AI CHAT LOG

Prompt

Describe the sections of a report and create an outline of what is typically included within each section.

ChatGPT

A report typically includes several structured sections to ensure clarity, coherence, and completeness. Here are the main parts of a report:

1. Title Page

2. Abstract/Executive Summary

3. Table of Contents

4. Introduction

5. Literature Review (if applicable)

6. Methodology

7. Results/Findings

8. Discussion

9. Conclusion

10. Recommendations (if not included in Conclusion)

11. References

12. Appendices

13. Glossary (if applicable)

You won't always need all of these sections, and your workplace may use a different format. While this report outline follows a typical research-based IMRAD format (introduction, methods, results, and discussion), there are several valid ways to write reports that don't follow this formal structure. For example, many types of business reports will not need a Literature Review or a Methods section. You may not need to include Recommendations, even as part of a conclusion because informational reports do not always give advice on what to do next. You should tailor your report sections to the topic at hand and decide what to leave in or leave out based on what your readers want and what the situation calls for.

The example scenario provided in this chapter demonstrates how to apply the three AI-writing methods to a type of section that commonly appears in reports: the introduction section. As I often point out to my business and technical writing students, an introduction is different from an executive summary or abstract. Introduction sections cover the background, purpose, and scope of a project. In contrast, executive summaries or abstracts capture key points from across all the document's sections, from introduction to conclusion.

For this demonstration, I'm using a sample report

published in 1919 by the United States Department of the Interior titled, "Business Education in Secondary Schools: A Report of the Commission on the Reorganization of Secondary Education, Appointed by the National Education Association." I'm using this report because its copyright has expired and because it will be interesting to see how ChatGPT critiques language that was used over a century ago. I demonstrate these methods so you can apply them to your own subject matter.

When writing prompts, it is a good idea to state your genre, audience, and purpose unless it is already implied. That way, AI understands the writing situation. You should also give AI a role that you want it to play.

Report Introduction with Method 1: Human-First Draft

For this method I'm taking the existing introduction to the report and asking ChatGPT to offer a revision. I also ask ChatGPT to explain the rationale for the revision.

AI CHAT LOG

Prompt

I would like you to act as a business writing tutor. I will give you a draft of a report introduction. A report introduction should include the following information: background, purpose, scope, and overview of methodology used to analyze data. If there is any missing information, insert placeholder text where I can provide details.

Please give me suggestions to improve this introduction, keeping my original voice. In your response, consider the following context, audience, and purpose of my report.

Context: I am on a commission that has been charged with reporting on the state of business education in secondary schools.

Audience: I am writing to government officials and the US public.

Purpose: The report introduction should set up the background, purpose, and scope of this project.

At the end of your suggested revision, explain what you changed from the original draft and why. When you are ready, please ask me for my draft text.

After ChatGPT responds that it is ready, I continue by pasting in the draft text.

Input text (original introduction and outline)

INTRODUCTION:

Sixteen years have elapsed since a committee of the business education department of the National Education Association submitted a report on the commercial curriculum with somewhat detailed treatment of the various subjects of study. Four years ago another committee of the same department made a less complete report. Subsequent changes in education and in business now call for further changes in commercial education in secondary schools.

The plan of the Commission on the Reorganization of Secondary Education offered an opportunity for a study of the secondary commercial curriculum in its relation to the other fields of secondary education. Early in the work of the commission a committee on business education was appointed under the chairmanship of Dr. A. L. Pugh, of the High School of Commerce, New York City. This committee made preliminary studies which were a contribution toward the present report. The present committee was organized in 1916, and consisted almost entirely of persons directly engaged in commercial education in secondary schools. Since the organization of the committee two members have been called to superintendencies of schools in large cities, and a third has been selected to assume the di-rection of commercial education for the Federal Board for Vocational Education.

An examination of the report will indicate that, while it has retained and given full credit to the earlier aspects of commercial education in which the aim was the training of bookkeepers and stenographers, there has been an enlargement of the field so that commercial education may take into its purview the preparation of salesmen and of those who are to participate in the broader aspects of business life.

The report contained in this bulletin has been approved not only by the committee on business education, but also by the reviewing committee of the commission. Approval by the reviewing committee does not commit every member individually to every statement and every implied educational doctrine, but does mean essential agreement as a committee with the general recommendations. Messrs. Inglis and Kingsley, of the reviewing committee, however, take exception to the limited amount of required social study suggested for years 9, 10, and 11, and in particular to the restrictions of community civics to two and one-half periods per week in the ninth year.

Attention is called to Bulletin 34 of the Federal Board of Vocational Education, entitled "Commercial Education: Organization and Administration." That bulletin, which was prepared by F. G. Nichols, who is a member of the committee on business education, is in a sense supplementary to the report in this bulletin. It contains an analysis of the various types of commercial education now needed, and indicates the part which Federal, State, and local agencies should take in the development and support of such education. It gives plans for the organization of secondary commercial education, devoting special attention to commercial work conducted in part-time, continuation, and evening classes.

OUTLINE: Part I. — The commercial curriculum : 1. The problem 11 2. Types of organization giving secondary commercial education 12 3. Purposes 1-i 4. Suggestions for a commercial curriculum 15 5. Need for definiteness of aim IS 6. Relations of commercial education to the business community 19 7. Educational aims of commercial curriculums 20 8. The short curriculum considered 21 9. Commercial work in the seventh, eighth, and ninth years 23 10. Suiting the curriculum to community *needs 24 Part II. — Suggestions regarding courses in the commercial curriculum: 1. English -C 2. Foreign languages ^0 3. Science ^^ 4. Social studies 32 5. Commercial studies 39 Part III. — Conclusion ^ Appendix ^'*

ChatGPT

INTRODUCTION

Sixteen years have passed since the business education department of the National Education Association last reported on the commercial curriculum in detail. Four years ago, another committee provided a less comprehensive update. With significant changes in both education and business over the past few years, a fresh look at commercial education in secondary schools is necessary.

The Commission on the Reorganization of Secondary Education saw an opportunity to evaluate the secondary commercial curriculum's relationship with other educational fields. Early on, Dr. A. L. Pugh, from the High School of Commerce in New York City, led a committee to conduct preliminary studies, contributing to this current report. Formed in 1916, our committee primarily consists of individuals directly involved in secondary commercial education. Since then, two members have taken on superintendencies in large city schools, and another has joined the Federal Board for Vocational Education to oversee commercial education.

This report builds on earlier efforts, which focused on training bookkeepers and stenographers, by expanding the scope to include preparing salespeople and others for broader business roles. The contents have been approved by both the committee on business education and the reviewing committee of the commission. While not every member agrees with each detail, there is general consensus on the recommendations. Notably, Inglis and Kingsley from the reviewing committee disagree with the limited required social studies in years 9, 10, and 11, and the restriction of community civics to two and a half periods per week in the ninth year.

For further context, refer to Bulletin 34 from the Federal Board of Vocational Education, titled "Commercial Education: Organization and Administration," prepared by committee member F. G. Nichols.

This supplementary bulletin analyzes current needs in commercial education and outlines the roles of Federal, State, and local agencies in its development and support. It also provides plans for organizing secondary commercial education, with special attention to part-time, continuation, and evening classes.

Changes and Reasoning:

1. Clarity and Brevity: Simplified some sentences to improve clarity and make the text more concise. For instance, "Four years ago another committee of the same department made a less complete report" was changed to "Four years ago, another committee provided a less comprehensive update."

2. Consistency: Used consistent time references ("Sixteen years have passed" instead of "Sixteen years have elapsed").

3. Flow: Improved the flow by reordering some information. For example, mentioning the formation of the current committee right after discussing Dr. Pugh's preliminary studies.

4. Expansion on Scope: Clarified the expansion of the curriculum scope from just training bookkeepers and stenographers to preparing salespeople and others for broader business roles.

5. Approval Details: Simplified the explanation about the approval of the report by the committee and the reviewing committee, emphasizing general consensus despite some disagreements.

6. Bulletin Reference: Made the reference to Bulletin 34 more straightforward and clearly linked it to the current report's context.

ChatGPT's version improves the readability of the text but in the process also alters the original voice, which had used a lot of prepositional phrases. The first version feels old-fashioned and wordy, reflecting characteristics that Richard Lanham (1979/2007) associates with the "official style." This bureaucratic and pompous way of writing over-relies on prepositions and prefers the verb "to be" instead of active verbs. Even though the official style is not very reader friendly, you still get the feeling that a human has written the report.

If I really had wanted to retain the original old-fashioned voice here, then ChatGPT failed to deliver. ChatGPT changed the voice even though I had instructed it not to. But is the sense of human presence still there? To a degree, but I need to read the revision aloud and adapt the text to resemble the voice that I have in mind.

ChatGPT's response also failed to follow the instructions about scope and methodology. When I read through the revised text, I notice that these aspects of the introduction have not been improved. After I asked ChatGPT if it addressed scope and methodology in its revision, it revised the output again to include those elements.

Revising my prompt and entering the instructions again could help to retain the original voice. For example, I could explain to ChatGPT what "voice" means as I had done in other prompts. I also could more explicitly define what scope and methodology mean in the original prompt.

This method seems effective for improving the readability of the report text. However, the results here underscore how important it is to carefully check AI outputs.

Report Introduction with Method 2: AI-Outlined Draft

When using the AI-Outlined Method, also use prompts that give ChatGPT a role to play as well as the details about my context, audience, and purpose.

Prompt

I would like you to act as a business writing tutor. Give me an outline for a report introduction that I want to write. Use brackets as placeholders where I should insert relevant information. Do not write the report introduction for me—just give me instructions and an outline for how to structure it. Also provide topic sentences for each paragraph. Below is my context, audience, and purpose.

Context: I am on a commission that has been charged with reporting on the state of business education in secondary schools.

Audience: I am writing to government officials and the US public.

Purpose: The report introduction should set up the background, purpose, and scope of this project.

ChatGPT

Outline for Report Introduction

1. Opening Paragraph: Introduce the Context

   - Topic Sentence: Business education in secondary schools is a critical component of preparing students for the modern workforce.

   - Instructions:

   - Begin with a strong statement about the importance of business education in secondary schools.

   - Provide a brief overview of the current state of business education in the US.

   - Highlight any relevant statistics or studies that underscore the need for this report.

2. Background Information

   - Topic Sentence: The landscape of business education has evolved significantly over the past decade.

- *Instructions:*

  - *Provide historical context on how business education has developed in secondary schools.*

  - *Mention key changes, trends, and milestones in the field.*

  - *Reference significant policies or educational reforms that have impacted business education.*

3. *Purpose of the Report*

  - *Topic Sentence: This report aims to provide a comprehensive analysis of the current state of business education in secondary schools.*

  - *Instructions:*

    - *Clearly state the main objectives of the report.*

    - *Explain why this report is necessary at this time.*

    - *Mention any specific issues or challenges that the report will address.*

4. *Scope of the Report*

  - *Topic Sentence: The scope of this report encompasses several key areas of business education.*

  - *Instructions:*

    - *Outline the main areas that the report will cover (e.g., curriculum, teaching methods, student outcomes, resource allocation).*

    - *Indicate the geographical focus (e.g., national, regional, or local levels).*

    - *Specify any limitations or areas that will not be covered in this report.*

5. *Importance of the Report*

  - *Topic Sentence: Understanding the current state of business education is crucial for informed decision-making and policy development.*

  - *Instructions:*

- *Discuss the potential impact of the report on stakeholders (e.g., students, educators, policymakers).*

- *Highlight the benefits of improving business education in secondary schools.*

- *Conclude with a statement about the anticipated outcomes or next steps following the report.*

Summary of Topic Sentences

1. *Business education in secondary schools is a critical component of preparing students for the modern workforce.*

2. *The landscape of business education has evolved significantly over the past decade.*

3. *This report aims to provide a comprehensive analysis of the current state of business education in secondary schools.*

4. *The scope of this report encompasses several key areas of business education.*

5. *Understanding the current state of business education is crucial for informed decision-making and policy development.*

I think this outline seems appropriate and covers all of the parts of a report introduction. I could envision myself using it while I write the report introduction. I would take special care when using the suggested topic sentences because I want to make sure that they come across in my voice.

Report Introduction with Method 3: AI-First Draft

Note that this prompt still has the core instructions from Methods 1 and 2. I give ChatGPT the details about my context, audience, and purpose, but I ask it to draft the report introduction for me.

AI CHAT LOG

Prompt

I would like you to act as a business writing tutor. Give me a draft of a report introduction that reflects my writing voice. I will give you my organization's voice sample as well as the report's table of contents.

The report has the following context, audience, and purpose.

Context: I am on a commission that has been charged with reporting on the state of business education in secondary schools.

Audience: I am writing to government officials and the US public.

Purpose: The report introduction should set up the background, purpose, and scope of this project.

When you are ready, prompt me for my organization's voice sample and the report's table of contents.

For my organization's voice sample, I pasted in a few sentences from the U.S. Government's style guide voice sample (see https://guides.18f.gov/content-guide/our-style/voice-and-tone/). For the table of contents, I pasted in the same outline that I had used in previous prompts.

Chat GPT

Introduction

Welcome to our report on the state of business education in secondary schools. This document is designed to serve as a comprehensive overview for government officials and the broader US public who are keen to understand and improve the commercial curriculum offered to our students.

Background

Business education in secondary schools is a vital component of our educational system, preparing students not just for further education but also for immediate entry into the workforce. Given the rapid changes in the business world, it's essential that our commercial curricula keep pace with these developments to provide relevant and practical education.

Purpose

The purpose of this report is to examine the current state of business education, identify areas for improvement, and offer practical suggestions for enhancing the curriculum. We aim to create a robust framework that aligns educational goals with the needs of the business community and the aspirations of our students.

Scope

This report is divided into three main parts:

1. The Commercial Curriculum: Here, we discuss the existing problems, the types of organizations providing secondary commercial education, the purposes of such education, and suggestions for curriculum improvements. We also explore the relationship between commercial education and the business community, aiming to ensure that the curriculum meets both educational and professional needs.

2. Suggestions Regarding Courses in the Commercial Curriculum: This section offers detailed recommendations for specific courses within the commercial curriculum, including English, foreign languages, science, social studies, and commercial studies. Our goal is to ensure that each subject contributes effectively to the overall educational objectives.

3. Conclusion: We wrap up with a summary of our findings and final thoughts, emphasizing the importance of a well-defined and community-oriented commercial curriculum.

Additionally, the appendix provides supplementary information and resources for further reference.

We hope this report serves as a useful guide and a call to action for all stakeholders involved in shaping the future of business education in our secondary schools.

ChatGPT did a decent job at structuring this introduction. To build on it, I would first change the general descriptions in the narrative to be more tailored to the content of my report. Right now, the text is fairly generic and lacks the presence that comes from specific details and human voice. I would go through and read each sentence aloud, changing words and phrasings to match what feels more natural to me. For example, in the first paragraph, "who are keen to understand" does not feel authentic. I would say "who seek to understand" or "who want to understand."

I thought ChatGPT's introduction was too short to warrant so many headings. However, some readers will always appreciate headings, even when the sections under them are brief. Plain language styles also tend to favor short paragraphs under multiple headings. Unless you tell it otherwise, ChatGPT will overuse headings and bulleted lists. So, if you use this Method 3 and want your text to read more like a cohesive narrative, you should prompt ChatGPT to not use headings and lists, or you can take them out as you revise.

Certain report sections are particularly suitable for AI assistance—for example, abstracts and executive summaries. To draft these kinds of sections, you can upload a

PDF of a draft to ChatGPT or another app and prompt it to write a summary. You can specify how short or long you want the summary to be by asking for a certain word count. This AI-generated summary can be a good starting point if you are struggling to concisely capture all the main points of a document. However, it is crucial to always doublecheck what AI gives you. AI likely will leave out important points or give weight to some points that aren't really that important. Always compare your own notes and ideas to the AI outputs.

When writing reports with AI, use a section-by-section approach and use a combination of the three methods. Asking AI for an outline (Method 2) could be useful when you are getting started, but there inevitably will be some sections that you will need to draft yourself using Method 1. When you get into the details of a topic or discuss findings, you naturally will express nuances in your thinking that AI is likely to miss—Method 1 is best for these types of sections. In contrast, Method 3 may be a good starting point for sections that involve informational overviews, such as introductions, executive summaries, and abstracts.

References

Lanham, R.A. (2007). *Revising Prose*. Originally published 1979.

Key Points

- Break up longer documents into sections when working with AI.
- Ask AI or consult open-source business writing textbooks if you aren't sure what should go in a specific type of document.
- Certain report sections are particularly suitable for AI assistance—for example, abstracts and executive summaries.
- Use a combination of the three methods when writing reports with AI.

The Future of Voice

Recently, ChatGPT rolled out an enhanced voice feature where users can choose to hear outputs in a variety of spoken voice styles. It seems that developers are continually improving AI avatars to sound more and more like humans. These new AI voices can sound convincing, especially if you only hear them once.

However, if you listen to enough AI-generated spoken voices from the same app, you'll start to notice not only peculiar intonations but also underlying patterns that aren't quite human. For example, Google's NotebookLM has "Deep Dive" podcast voices that sound unique and possibly human the first time you listen. But when I listened to multiple "Deep Dives," I noticed that the same phrases and intonations started to repeat regardless of the topic at hand. I also noticed repetitive patterns when conversing with ChatGPT's enhance voice model. The voice avatar always would ask me a leading question after it responded to my previous statement. I'm sure that at some point developers will figure out how to vary these patterns to make AI writing and speech more humanlike.

What does that mean for writing and communication? On the plus side, voice avatars that deliver AI-generated translations will improve cross-cultural communication. Information will become more accessible to many people. At the same time, when people don't know that they are interacting with an AI avatar, there's a lot of potential for abuse and misinformation.

There are many other ethical problems that have come with advancements in generative AI. The processing power that it takes to run this technology is consuming more energy than ever. LLMs also perpetuate human biases and can reinforce discriminatory practices. Societies and governments will need to figure out how to address these problems and pass laws that protect people and the environment. Hopefully, future advances in AI science also will lead to solutions.

When it comes to generative AI for writing, I don't think that products like ChatGPT, Gemini, or Claude will ever be able to fully replicate the sense of voice or human presence that comes across when people write or speak. What we call AI is not sentient (at least not yet), and it lacks the capacity to feel and convey emotion. AI tools can be creative aids to our writing processes, but we will always need human writers who can empathize with audiences.

Every person who writes, even if it's just for routine business purposes, is a writer with a unique voice. We can't allow AI to change that. I hope that this book has inspired you to be more aware of your own voice when you use generative AI and feel more confident about your writing.